Discovering Religions

HINDUISM

Sue Penney

RSVP
RAINTREE
STECK-VAUGHN
PUBLISHERS
The Steck-Vaughn Company

Austin, Texas

Published by Raintree Steck-Vaughn Publishers, an imprint of Steck-Vaughn Company

Library of Congress Cataloging-in-Publication Data

Penney, Sue.
Hinduism / Sue Penney.
   p. cm. — (Discovering religions)
Includes index.
Summary: Discusses the origins, history, and practice of Hinduism, including information about various festivals and celebrations.
   ISBN 0-8172-4397-6
   1. Hinduism—Juvenile literature.   [1. Hinduism.]
BL1203.H56 1997
294.5—dc20   96-6981
                                              CIP
                                               AC

Religious Studies consultants: W. Owen Cole and Steven L. Ware (Drew University)

Thanks are due to V P (Hemant) Kanitkar for reading and advising on the manuscript.

Designed by Visual Image
Illustrated by Visual Image
Typeset by Tom Fenton Studio
Cover design by Amy Atkinson

Printed in Great Britain

1 2 3 4 5 6 7 8 9 WO 99 98 97 96

Acknowledgments
The publishers would like to thank the following for permission to use photographs:

Cover photograph by Comstock.

The Ancient Art and Architecture Collection p. 8; Andes Press Agency p. 24; Mohamed Ansar/Impact Photos pp. 32, 43; The Bridgeman Art Library p. 12; The J. Allan Cash Photo Library p. 27; Circa Photo Library pp. 17, 22, 29, 36, 40 (left); Comstock p. 26; Douglas Dickins pp. 15, 20; C M Dixon p. 18; Ben Edwards/Impact Photos p. 41; Sally and Richard Greenhill pp. 16, 44 (below), 45; Sunil Gupta/ Network p. 33; Ian Happs pp. 10, 19; Judy Harrison/Format Partners p. 34; The Hutchison Library pp. 28, 42, 47; Roshini Kempadoo/ Format Partners p. 40 (right); Christine Osborne Pictures   p. 6; Ann and Bury Peerless pp. 9, 11, 13, 14, 30, 31, 46; Sarita Sharma/Format Partners p. 44 (top); Topham Picturepoint pp. 21, 25, 35, 38, 39.

The author and publishers would like to thank the following for permission to use material for which they hold copyright: Columbia University Press for the extract from *Sources of Indian Tradition,* edited by William T. de Bary, 1958, on p. 19; J. M. Dent for the extract from *Hindu Scriptures,* translated and edited by R. C. Zaehner, 1972, on p. 7; Grafton Books for the extract from a radio broadcast by Jawaharlal Nehru, quoted in *Freedom at Midnight* by Larry Collins and Dominique Lapierre, 1982, on p. 39; V P (Hemant) Kanitkar for the extracts from *Discovering Sacred Texts: Hindu Scriptures,* published by Heinemann Educational, 1994, on pp. 11, 17, 23, 31, 33, 37, 41, 43, 45, 47; Hodder and Stoughton for the extracts from *Hindu Belief and Practice* by Damodar Sharma, 1984, on pp. 9, 21, 29; Stanley Thornes (Publishers) Ltd for the extract from the Bhagavad Gita taken from *Five World Religions in the Twentieth Century* by W Owen Cole, 1981, on p. 15; Penguin Books Ltd for the extracts from *The Upanishads,* translated and selected by Juan Mascaro, 1965, on pp. 27, 35; *The Seabury Press* for the extract from The Smokeless Fire, edited by Catherine Hughes, 1974, on p. 13.

The publishers have made every effort to trace copyright holders. However, if any material has been incorrectly acknowledged, we would be pleased to correct this at the earliest opportunity.

CONTENTS

MAP: WHERE THE MAIN RELIGIONS BEGAN

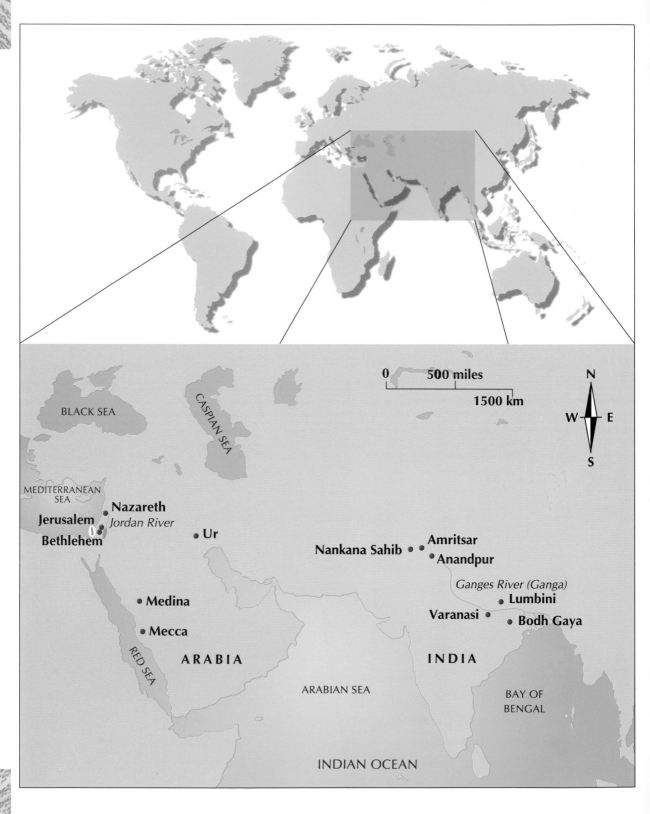

0   500 miles
     1500 km

N
W — E
S

BLACK SEA

CASPIAN SEA

MEDITERRANEAN
SEA

Nazareth
Jerusalem
Jordan River
Bethlehem

• Ur

Nankana Sahib • • Amritsar
                 • Anandpur

Ganges River (Ganga)

• Medina   • Lumbini
                      Varanasi • • Bodh Gaya
• Mecca

RED SEA

ARABIA   INDIA

ARABIAN SEA   BAY OF
                    BENGAL

INDIAN OCEAN

4

TIME CHART: WHEN THE MAIN RELIGIONS BEGAN

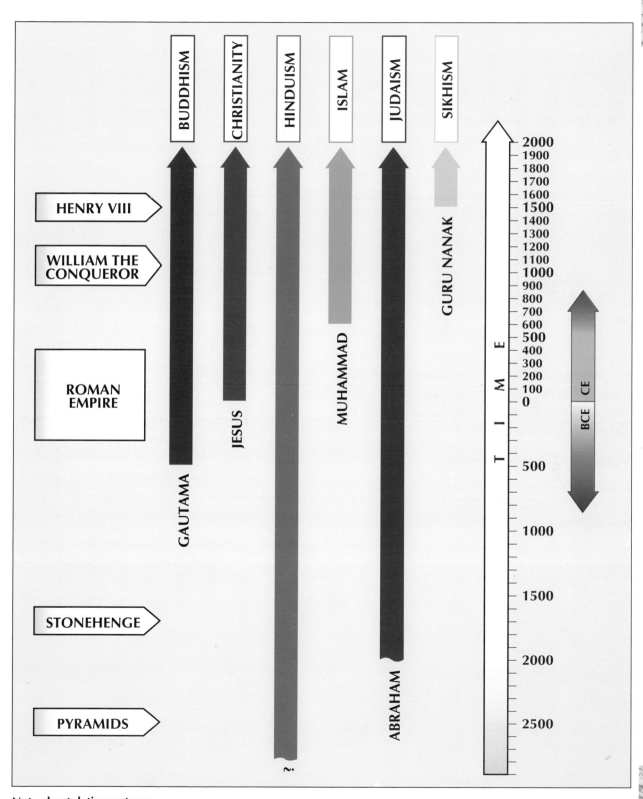

Note about dating systems

In this book dates are not called BC and AD which is the Christian dating system. The letters BCE and CE are used instead. BCE stands for Before the Common Era and CE stands for Common Era. BCE and CE can be used by people of all religions, Christians too. The year numbers are not changed.

INTRODUCING HINDUISM

This section tells you something about who Hindus are.

Hinduism is the oldest of the major world religions. It began so long ago that no one really knows how old it is, but it goes back at least 5,000 years. The name "Hindu" comes from an old name for people who lived in part of northern India. Today, over 800 million people living in India are Hindus, and at least as many live in other parts of the world.

Hinduism was not begun by any one person, and it developed gradually over more than a thousand years. This means that today it has many different branches, and its followers have a very wide range of beliefs and ways of worshiping. Hinduism is a way of life as much as a religion. Different Hindus may believe quite different things without being "right" or "wrong." This book concentrates on things that almost all Hindus would agree with.

What do Hindus believe?

Hindus who know the Holy Scriptures well prefer to call it **Sanatan dharma**. This means **eternal** truths—in other words, basic teachings that have always been true and always will be. These truths are written about in the Hindu holy books called the **Vedas**. Some of the books contain hymns to be used in worship, others are discussions about important issues. Orthodox Hindus believe that following the teachings of these books is the most important part of their faith.

Hinduism teaches that there is one Great Power. This is not a person, and not "he" or "she," but "it." It is called **Brahman**. Many Hindus would say Brahman can be translated as "God." It is everywhere, and everything that exists lives in Brahman all the time. Nothing would exist if God was not in it. Hindus often explain this by using an example. They say that it is like salt dissolved in water. The salt is present even in the tiniest drop of the water and makes it what it is. In the same way, God is in everything in the universe, and this makes everything what it is. Many Hindus say that this power can be seen most easily through gods. The three main gods are Shiva, Vishnu, and Brahma.

Hindu children worshiping at home.

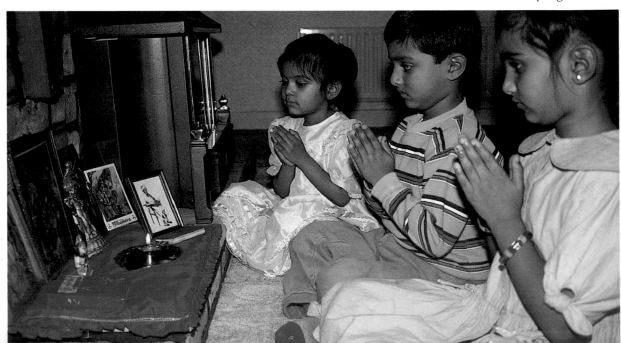

Reincarnation

Another important part of Hindu belief is the idea of **reincarnation**. This is the belief that when you die, your **soul** goes on to live in another person, animal, or other being. Where it goes depends on how you have lived in this life. The aim of every Hindu is to become good enough to break out of this cycle of birth and death, so that their soul can become part of Brahman. This will be perfect happiness.

The Hindu symbol "Oum."

Symbols of Hinduism

The **symbol** often used for Hinduism is the **sacred** sound **"Oum"** written in Sanskrit. (Sanskrit is a very old language, in which the Hindu holy books were first written.) Before they were written, they were remembered by chanting for generations. Hindus believe the world is filled with the sound and energy of Oum. By sitting in a certain yoga position and chanting "Oum" in a certain way, the worshiper can absorb the cosmic energy.

HINDU TEACHING

This passage comes from one of the Hindu holy books. It sums up much Hindu teaching.

Speak the truth.

Do what is right.

Do not neglect study of the Vedas ...

Do not be careless about what is right.

Do not be careless about welfare.

Do not be careless about prosperity ...

Perform only deeds to which no blame attaches, no others ...

Give with faith: do not give without faith.

Give plentifully: give modestly:

Give with awe: give with sympathy.

Taittiriya Upanishad 11.1–2

GODS AND GODDESSES 1

This section tells you about the most important Hindu gods.

There are thousands of gods and goddesses in Hinduism. When the religion began, the people probably believed that these gods and goddesses really existed. Some Hindus may still believe this, but today most Hindus agree that the gods are not real beings. They are seen as symbols for describing Brahman, the Great Power. Brahman is beyond the understanding of human beings, so the gods and goddesses are ways of showing something that cannot be described. Hindus believe that if they worship Brahman through a god or goddess they can understand, they will find it easier to worship properly.

Trimurti

There are three gods that Hindus believe are the most important. They are Brahma the **creator**, Vishnu the **preserver,** and Shiva the destroyer. These three gods are known as the **Trimurti**. They work together in a never-ending pattern. Everything is made, lasts for a time, and is then destroyed. This section concentrates on Vishnu and Shiva because today they are worshiped much more than Brahma.

Vishnu

Vishnu is worshiped under several different names. This is because of his different incarnations, or appearances. Hindus believe that when there is a time of danger for the earth, Vishnu comes to protect it. They believe he has come to earth in ten different bodies, some animal, like a fish or turtle, and some human. Two of these appearances are much more important than the others. One was when he came as the god Rama, and the other when he came as the god Krishna.

Rama's story is told in the poem called the Ramayana (see page 15), which is part of the Hindu holy books. He was a prince whose wife was captured by an evil demon. The story includes many adventures before in the end good wins over evil. Krishna is the hero of the Bhagavad Gita, part of a poem called the Mahabharata. (See page 14.) He is very important, and is worshiped by more Hindus than any other god.

Shiva

Shiva is worshiped by about a quarter of all Hindus. He is the god of procreation, or reproduction, and the god who destroys. So he

An old statue showing Vishnu with Brahma and Shiva.

Shiva, the Lord of the Dance.

controls life and death. Although he can be frightening, he is also thought of as being kind and easy to please. Shiva destroys things that are old or no longer needed, but this allows new things to happen. He has at least four hands to show that he holds life and death and good and evil. He is often shown as the Lord of the Dance, and his dance is the energy that keeps the universe moving. Sometimes he is shown dancing on a monster that he is destroying. The monster is ignorance.

Many Hindu gods and goddesses have several different names that show different parts of their character. This can be quite confusing, even for Hindus. The important thing to remember is that all the gods and goddesses are ways of describing Brahman the Great Power.

NEW WORDS

Creator One who makes things.
Preserver One who keeps things from decay.
Trimurti The three gods—Brahma, Vishnu, and Shiva.

A PRAYER IN PRAISE OF VISHNU

I bow down to you Oh God Vishnu, the Lord of the universe, the Lord of all demigods, the sustainer of the universe, who are present everywhere like space, with a complexion like the color of clouds, handsome and well-proportioned limbs and eyes like lotus petals; who are capable of freeing people from the miseries of the world and who can be realized in meditation only by those who practice yoga.

Sukti Sudhakar v 106

GODS AND GODDESSES II

This section tells you about some of the Hindu gods and goddesses who are worshipped most often.

A Hindu can choose to worship any of the thousands of gods or goddesses, or more than one. Their choice often depends on which gods their family worship, or perhaps on an event where they believe one particular god has helped them. Some gods and goddesses are particularly popular.

Shakti

Many of the gods have "families," and one of the most popular goddesses is Shiva's wife. Like many Hindu gods and goddesses, she has more than one name to show different parts of her personality. She is sometimes called Shakti, the

Mother Goddess. In other forms she is called Durga or Kali or Parvati. As Durga, she destroys demons. As Kali, she is often pictured wearing a necklace of skulls, with six or eight hands holding weapons. She is often shown dancing with Shiva. Although she is frightening, Kali is seen as giving peace to her followers because she helps them overcome their fears. As Parvati, however, she is peace-loving and gentle.

Lakshmi

Lakshmi is the wife of Vishnu. She is the goddess of beauty and wealth, and of good fortune. She is not as important as Durga, but many Hindus pray to her especially at New Year, asking that the financial year to come will be a good one for them.

Kali.

Ganesha

Ganesha is the god of wisdom and strength and preventer of obstacles. In the "god-family," Ganesha is Shiva's son. The stories say that Shiva cut off Ganesha's head by mistake when he was in a temper. He gave Ganesha an elephant's head in its place. This is why Ganesha is always shown with an elephant's head.

Hanuman

Hanuman is the monkey god. He stands for intelligence. In the story of the Ramayana (see page 15), Hanuman helped the prince Rama when his wife Sita had been kidnapped.

Hinduism is a very tolerant religion. Hindus do not claim that the god they worship is the only right one—many of the holy books talk of worshiping more than one god. They also do not try to persuade other people to become Hindus. They believe that the most important thing is that each person should worship God in the way that he or she feels to be right for them.

Ganesha.

PRAYER TO GANESHA

Ganesha is the elephant-headed god of wisdom and strength. Many Hindus worship him every day because he is believed to be the god who can remove problems. This is a typical prayer offered to Ganesha:

We call upon you, Ganesha, the leader of the assembly of Gods, the divine priest, the scholar among scholars, first among the knowers of Brahman, of incomparable fame. Hear our prayer and grace this place with your all-protecting presence.

Rig-Veda 2.23.1

HOLY BOOKS I

This section tells you about the most important Hindu holy books.

Hinduism has developed over thousands of years. Many different books have been written during that time. These include books about the gods, the correct way to worship, and Hindu beliefs. Most of these holy books are written in Sanskrit, one of the oldest languages in the world. Today it is only used for religious purposes. Some of these books are not often read today, but others are still very important.

The Vedas

The Vedas are the oldest of the Hindu holy books. Hindus believe that the Vedas came from God, and they contain basic truths that never change. They go back to about 1200 BCE, but they were not collected and written down until the early centuries of the Common Era. The teachings were passed down by word of mouth. A father would teach his son the words, the son taught his son, and so on. People in those days were used to remembering things, because very few people could read or write.

The most important Veda is the first. It is called the **Rig Veda**, and contains over 1,000 hymns. They are made up of verses called **mantras**. The hymns are really poems praising the 33 gods who control the forces of nature. The other Vedas contain instructions to the priests about how worship should be carried out, and descriptions of religious ceremonies.

The Upanishads

The Upanishads are the last part of each Veda. The name comes from words that mean "sit down near," and this is how the teachings began. People who wanted to learn from wise men would sit down around them, listen to what they said, and learn from it. The Upanishads contain discussions about the most important things which Hindus believe, for example, what God is like, and how human beings can know God.

The Laws of Manu

The Laws of Manu are some of the most important law books for Hindus. No one really knows when Manu lived, but he was a wise

Sanskrit, a page from an illustrated copy of the Madhandoya Purana.

teacher whose words were written down by 300 CE. There are 2,685 verses in the books of the Laws of Manu. They contain instructions about how Hindus should live their lives, and show how important it is to follow the teachings of Hinduism in everyday life. They include the punishments for certain crimes, and rules that priests should follow.

The Puranas

The Puranas were written down over a period of about a thousand years, after about 500 CE. The word *puranas* means olden times. They are part of the group of holy books that help to explain the Vedas. They contain many well-known stories, and deal mainly with the wor-

*Reading the holy books is
an important part of Hindu worship.*

ship of Brahma, Vishnu, Shiva, and Shakti. Altogether there are over half a million verses in the Puranas.

BRAHMAN

This is part of a passage in one of the Upanishads that describes Brahman.

> *In the beginning this world was Brahman, the limitless One— limitless to the east, limitless to the south, limitless to the west, limitless to the north, and above and below, limitless in every direction. Truly, for him east and other directions exist not, nor across, nor below, nor above. Incomprehensible is that supreme soul, unlimited, unborn, not to be reasoned about, unthinkable—he whose soul is space!*

Maitri Upanishad

HOLY BOOKS II

This section tells you about two important Hindu poems.

There are two long poems that form part of the Hindu holy books. One is called the Mahabharata, and the other is called the Ramayana. They are important not just because they are good stories, but also because of the lessons they teach about the religion.

The Mahabharata

The *Mahabharata* is the longest poem in the world. It has 100,000 verses! It was not written by one person, but was added to by many people over several hundred years. The poem is complicated because, in addition to the main story, it has many other stories that are included to teach important lessons. The main story is about two royal families. They are cousins and quarrel over who should be the rightful ruler of the country. One family tricks the other, and war begins. There is a great battle. Before the battle begins, one of the royal princes, Arjuna, puts his arms down and tells his chariot driver and advisor, Lord Krishna, that he cannot fight. The battle is against his cousins, teachers, and other respected elders. Krishna convinces Arjuna that he must do his duty. He reasons with him why one must do his or her duties, even if they are unpleasant. This is the most often read portion of this scripture and is called "The Bhagavad Gita," the Song of the Lord. In this way Krishna teaches the prince about his duty and about the right ways for people to worship. The Bhagavad Gita is also the most important part of the Scriptures for many Hindus.

This painting shows Krishna and Arjuna before the battle.

14

Dancing the Ramayana (Rama faces Ravana, Hanuman is on the right).

The Ramayana

The *Ramayana* has 24,000 verses. It is thought to be the work of a man called Valmiki, and was probably written down in about 100 CE. It tells the story of Prince Rama and his wife Sita. Prince Rama was an incarnation, or appearance, of the god Vishnu. In the story, Rama's father has promised his youngest wife two wishes. She asks for her own son to be made king instead of Rama, and for Rama to be sent away for fourteen years. The king is heartbroken, but has to keep his promise. Rama obeys his father, and with his wife and his brother goes to live in the forest. While they are there, Rama's wife Sita is kidnapped by the wicked demon, Ravana, who keeps her prisoner on an island. The monkey-god Hanuman helps Rama to find Sita, and Hanuman's monkey army helps Rama to win a fierce battle against Ravana. In the battle, Rama kills Ravana, and he and Sita are able to return home. Rama is crowned king. Good wins over evil.

The stories in the *Mahabharata* and the Ramayana can be understood on many different levels. For children, they are exciting stories. For adults, they teach important lessons about the gods and the way to worship. Many Hindu actors and dancers use parts of the stories in their performances.

FROM THE BHAGAVAD GITA

Whatever one offers me with true devotion—only a leaf or a flower, a fruit or even a little water—this I accept from a yearning soul because with a pure heart it was offered with love. Whatever you do or eat or give or offer in sacrifice, let it be an offering to me; and whatever you suffer, suffer it for me. Give me your mind and give me your heart, give me your offerings and your adoration; thus with your soul in harmony, and making me your supreme goal, you will in truth come to me.

Bhagavad Gita 9.26, 27, 34

WORSHIP I

This section tells you about how Hindus worship at home.

Hindus believe that their religion affects everything they do, so everything in their life is worship. Particular forms of worship may include repeating the names of God, listening to or reading the holy books or making offerings. The most common form of worship is called **puja**. This can take place at home or in the temple.

Puja

Puja can happen in many different ways—it may be very simple or very complicated. The rules for making puja are laid down in the Hindu holy books. It involves making offerings to an image or picture of one of the gods or goddesses. An image is called a **murti**, which means form. A murti is intended to help people worship, because it is a way of showing one of the qualities of Brahman.

A Hindu house always has a **shrine** where the murti, or pictures, are kept. A shrine is a special holy place. Sometimes it is very simple, just a shelf on the wall. Other shrines are beautifully decorated. If the house is large enough, the shrine will be in a separate room. If not, it is usually in the kitchen or the mother's bedroom. The murti is surrounded by flowers and perfume. Sometimes pictures of other gods or important Hindus are kept in the shrine too. There may also be a container of water taken from the Ganges River that Hindus believe is a sacred river.

Worship at home takes place at least once a day. The point of the worship is to spend time in the presence of God, so Hindus prepare for it and perform it very carefully. If there is a murti in the shrine, it is washed, dried, and touched with special colored powders. It may have

flowers hung around it. Food, water, and flowers are offered, but the gifts do not need to be large or expensive—a flower petal or a grain of rice is enough. While they are making puja, Hindus repeat mantras. These are usually verses from the holy books. They begin with the sacred word Oum, which may be used as a mantra on its own. Worshipers do not wear shoes, and

A Hindu woman worshiping at home.

they stand or sit cross-legged. They may put their hands together and lift them to their chest or forehead, or kneel and touch the ground in front of the murti with their forehead. These are all ways of showing respect.

Other worship

It is part of Hindu belief that God is in everything, so everything that a Hindu does in their life can be counted as worship. This means that even simple everyday tasks, like cooking a meal or washing up, can be part of worship if they are done properly and with care.

Meditation

Meditation is a way of training and controlling your mind. The aim is to concentrate on God so completely that you stop being aware of anything else, even yourself. Meditation is an important part of Hindu worship. There are instructions in the holy books for ways it can be done. In this book, it is explained in more detail on page 24.

In this book, it is explained in more detail on page 24.

NEW WORDS

Meditation Mental control, especially concentrating on God.
Murti Form—image of a god or goddess that has been specially blessed.
Puja Worship of a god or goddess.
Shrine Holy place.

A Hindu boy praying in front of a murti.

A PRAYER BEFORE PUJA

This prayer from the Puranas is often recited before making puja.

For success in all my actions I first praise Ganesha, my Guru, the Sun God, Brahma, Vishnu, Shiva, and Saraswati.

Homage to God Ganesha, remover of all obstacles, worshiped by both gods and demons in order to attain their desires.

May Brahma, Shiva, and Vishnu, the Lords of the three worlds, make us successful in everything.

WORSHIP II

This section tells you about Hindu worship in temples.

A Hindu temple is called a **mandir** or a temple. There are many different kinds of mandirs. Some are small and simple, especially in villages where the people are poor. Other mandirs may be very large and beautifully decorated, often with stone and wood carvings showing scenes from the life of the god. Many temples in India are built where the stories say that a god or goddess lived or appeared to people.

Large mandirs are something like small villages themselves. There is a main shrine room, and other rooms with shrines to gods who are not as important. Priests need to look after the temple, so there are rooms where they can live. There is always a river or other supply of water, so that people can wash before they go to worship. (This is a special washing to make the people fit for worship. It has nothing to do with being dirty.) Small temples are similar, but they do not have as many rooms. They may have just a shrine room and somewhere for the priest to live.

Worship in the mandir

All Hindu mandirs, even if they are very small, have at least one priest. It is his job to look after the murti and help the people to worship. Worship often begins before dawn. The murti is "woken up" and mantras beginning with the sacred word "Oum" are said. The murti is washed with cold water, dried, and has sandalwood paste applied to it. It may have flowers hung on it. If it has been "asleep" in a separate room, it is moved to the shrine room, and offerings are made to it. Worship may take place several times a day. Hindus believe that even the smallest murti should be worshiped at least once a day.

When worshipers arrive at the temple, they take off their shoes as a sign of respect. They give the gifts they have brought to the priest, who takes them into the shrine room. Ordinary people do not usually go into the shrine room except at festival time. The gifts may be small sums of money, but usually they are things like fruit, nuts, or flowers. The worship of some gods and goddesses includes a **sacrifice** of the life of an animal, but this is not usual.

The main tower of a temple in Madurai, India.

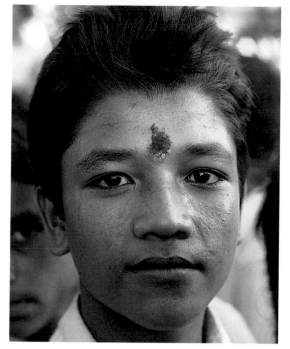

Tilak may show that the person has been to worship.

Hindus do not usually worship in groups, but in large temples the priest may sometimes offer prayers in front of a group of people. This worship usually includes three parts that may be put together. The first is **bhajan,** which is the singing of hymns, usually from the Vedas. Then there are two forms of worship that use fire. **Havan** means worshiping by making offerings to the god of fire. A fire is lit in a small altar, using small pieces of wood and **ghee** (clarified butter). Prayers are said as the fire burns. The other worship is called **arti**. A small tray containing five lights is slowly waved in front of the murti. Then it is taken among the people who are worshiping. Sometimes they put small gifts of money on the tray. They hold their hands over the flames, then wipe their hands over their head. They believe that by doing this they receive power from the god. Special hymns are sung.

During worship, people place a dot or stripes of special powder or sandlewood paste on their forehead. This is **tilak** (sometimes called tikka). It often shows that the person has been to worship. This is not the same as the red dot that many Hindu women place on their forehead, which just shows that they are married. Or sometimes it is just a decoration.

INSTRUCTIONS FOR WORSHIP

This passage is about the right way to worship.

> *When I am worshiped in an icon (murti), bathing Me and decorating Me are welcome. When worshiped in the sun, adoration by prostration, offering of water with mantras, muttering of prayer are best. Some water offered to Me with love by a devotee pleases Me. Elaborate offerings, sandal, incense, flowers, light, food, made by one who is devoid of devotion, do not satisfy Me.*

Bhagavata-Purana

NEW WORDS

Arti Worship using fire and lights.
Bhajan Hymn used in worship.
Ghee Clarified butter.
Havan Worship by making offerings to the god of fire.
Mandir Hindu temple.
Sacrifice Offering to a god or goddess.
Tilak Mark placed on the forehead.

PILGRIMAGE

This section tells you about some of the places where Hindus go on **pilgrimage**.

A pilgrimage is a journey that people make for religious reasons. Pilgrimages are often part of Hindu worship. Many Hindus feel that going on such a journey is part of their religious duty. There are many different reasons why people choose to go on pilgrimages. They may want to visit a place where the god they worship appeared to people, or where a **miracle** happened. Sometimes they want to pray for something special and believe that their prayer is more likely to be answered if they are in a holy place.

The Jaganath mandir at Puri.

Places for pilgrimage

There are hundreds of places for pilgrimage all over India. Pilgrims may go on a one-day visit to the nearest shrine, or a longer journey to a more important shrine or mandir. Four mandirs in India are often thought to be particularly important. These are thousands of miles apart at the four "corners" of India. Puri on the east coast, Dwarka on the west coast, and Badrinath in the north are shrines to Vishnu. Rameshwaram on the south coast is a shrine to Shiva. Many Hindus spend most of their lives saving up to be able to visit all of them. They may be poor and have great difficulties on the journey, but they believe that putting up with the hardships is part of serving God. For the same reason, some Hindus think that for a pilgrimage, it is better to walk. It may be hundreds of miles from where they live to the place they want to visit, and may take weeks or even months to walk there, but they believe that the effort makes the pilgrimage more worthwhile. When they arrive at the temple or shrine, many pilgrims crawl around it on their hands and knees. This is to show that they know they have done things in their life that are wrong, and they are sorry. The same sort of worship goes on at all the shrines that the pilgrims visit. They give presents to the god they have come to worship. These are the same kind of presents they would give in worship at home—food, flowers, money.

Holy rivers

Water is necessary for life, and many rivers are respected by Hindus because they believe they are a symbol of God who gives life. Bathing in a holy river is also important because it washes away **sin**—all the things that a person has done wrong in life. There are seven holy rivers in India, but the most famous is the Ganges River (also called the Ganga). Millions of Hindus bathe in its waters, and they believe that drinking even one drop of its water will get rid of all the sins they have committed in this life and in previous lives.

Varanasi

The most important place on the Ganges River is Varanasi, sometimes called Benares. This is where the god Shiva is supposed to have lived, and it is has been a center for religious teaching for thousands of years. There are special platforms called **ghats** with steps that allow pilgrims to get to the river to bathe or offer puja. Every Hindu hopes to be in Varanasi when they die, and some of the ghats are used for **cremating** dead bodies. After the body has been burned, the ashes will be scattered in the river. The ashes of people who have died elsewhere are often scattered there, too. Hindus believe that this will help the person to break out of the cycle of rebirth.

NEW WORDS

Cremate Burn a dead body.
Ghat Steps and platform on a river-bank.
Miracle Event that cannot be explained.
Pilgrimage Journey for religious reasons.
Sin Wrongdoing.

THE GANGES RIVER

This passage explains why Hindus think the Ganges River is so important.

> He who with reverence utters the holy name of Ganga, even if he is hundreds of miles away from it, gets absolved from all his sins and proceeds straight to the abode of Vishnu.
>
> O, Mother Ganga, I bow down to you, because by a mere touch of your holy waters, even snakes, horses, deer, and monkeys, as well as men, become as pure, as beautiful, and as adorned as Shiva.
>
> Gangashtaka Kalidasa 8

Worshipers bathing in the Ganges River at Varanasi.

HINDU BELIEF

This section tells you something about important Hindu beliefs.

Hinduism is more a way of life than a religion, and its followers do not all believe the same things. The beliefs studied in this unit are ones that almost all Hindus would agree are very important.

Dharma

Hindus believe that life involves a series of duties. These duties are called **dharma**. Dharma is not the same for every person because it depends on your family background, your job, and many other things. It includes things like worshiping God, doing your job properly, not hurting other people or animals, and being honest. It is up to every person to do their dharma as well as they possibly can. For Hindus, this is the first aim in life.

Reincarnation

Reincarnation is a very important part of Hindu teaching. It is the belief that when your body dies, your soul (Hindus call it **atman**) moves on to another being. The soul in everything is the same—there is no difference between the soul in a plant or animal and a human being. Hindus believe that the soul moves through a series of "steps." It begins in plants and animals and goes on to human beings. When a man or woman dies, the soul is rehoused in another person. This continual cycle of birth and death is called **samsara**.

Karma

The type of person your soul moves on to depends on how you have lived. This is called the law of **karma**. Karma means action. A good karma in your last life will mean a good life this time. A bad karma in your last life will mean a hard life this time. From this comes the belief that there is no point in complaining or being proud of the sort of life you lead. It all comes from the way you behaved in your last life, so it is your own responsibility.

Just as this life is decided by your last life, the way you live now will decide what happens next. There is no idea in Hinduism of being judged by God—this is not necessary. How you live will determine whether your next life is a step up or a step down. Steps may be skipped, depending on the karma. Some Hindus believe that doing something very bad will mean your soul is reborn in an animal and has to work its way up to a human being again. Doing something very good may mean your soul is given a rest before being reborn.

Dharma includes doing your job to the best of your ability.

BRAHMAN

The law of samsara.

NEW WORDS

Atman The soul in everything.
Dharma The duties of living.
Karma The actions that affect rebirth.
Moksha End of the rebirth cycle.
Samsara The law of rebirth.

REINCARNATION

This verse is part of the quotations from the Scriptures said over the body at a Hindu funeral. It describes reincarnation.

> May your sight be absorbed into the sun and your atman escape into the atmosphere. May your atman reach the region of light or once more return to earth, or perhaps go to the waters or to the plants, taking on new bodies, depending on the consequences of its actions.

Rig Veda 10.16.3

Moksha

The end of samsara is called **moksha**. It is what every Hindu hopes to achieve. The soul breaks out of the cycle of rebirth and joins with Brahman. Hindus say that this is like a river merging with the sea. This can only happen when the soul becomes completely pure and is not affected by anything that happens on earth. Then the soul can go back to being part of Brahman, where it began.

23

YOGAS

This section tells you about the different ways that Hindus try to achieve moksha.

Moksha is freedom from the cycle of rebirth. Hindus believe that the soul is rehoused in different bodies over and over again until moksha is achieved, and the soul can merge with Brahman. The Bhagavad Gita mentions four paths that lead to moksha. These are the paths of knowledge, meditation, devotion (love of a god or goddess), and action. Each path is open to anyone, and many Hindus use more than one path in their lives. They do not have to choose one and ignore the others.

The path of knowledge—Jnana-yoga

"Knowledge" in this sense means spiritual knowledge rather than just knowing a lot of things. Hindus who follow this path usually need a good teacher. They need to study the religion carefully, and they follow a pattern for their lives. This leads them to knowledge of the relationship between the soul (atman) and God (Brahman).

The path of meditation—Raja-yoga

For Hindus, meditation means concentrating so hard that you forget everything around you, and forget even yourself, so that you can reach the real self that is within you. This is the path that has given its name to what most people in Western countries think of as being yoga—the special positions and breathing exercises that clear your mind. The difficulty of this path is that it cannot be followed if you have responsibilities—you cannot concentrate if you are worrying about work or money or family. To ignore your responsibilities goes against Hindu teaching about doing your duty, and means that you would not gain any merit by meditating.

Young Hindus in a Western country learning about their religion.

Meditation.

The path of devotion—Bhakti-yoga

The path of devotion involves choosing a particular god or goddess and spending your whole life worshiping him or her. This means praying to the god or goddess, offering puja, going on pilgrimages, and making sure that all the actions in your life are an offering to him or her.

The path of good works—Karma-yoga

Many Hindus think that for ordinary people, the path of good works is the easiest one to follow. It involves doing your dharma—your duty—to the best of your ability. Dharma is not the same for every person, because it depends on what job you do, what social group you come from, and many other things.

The different yogas are all ways that Hindus may reach Brahman. Hindus do not think that any one path is better than the others, and many follow more than one yoga in their lives. The important thing is to reach Brahman in the end. Many Hindus say that it is like climbing a mountain—which path you choose is not important. Some paths may be steeper or harder to walk up, but different people have different abilities. So long as you reach the top, the achievement is the same—it does not matter how you got there.

ADVICE FOR PRACTICING YOGA

With upright body, head, and neck, lead the mind and its powers into your heart; and the Aum [Oum] of Brahman will then be your boat with which to cross the rivers of fear.

And when the body is in silent steadiness, breathe rhythmically through the nostrils with a peaceful ebbing and flowing of breath. The chariot of the mind is drawn by wild horses and those horses have to be tamed. Find a quiet retreat for the practice of Yoga, sheltered from the wind, level and clean, free from trash, smoldering fires, and ugliness, and where the sound of waters and the beauty of the place help thought and contemplation.

Svetasvatara Upanishad part 2

HINDU LIFE

This section looks at two ways that religion affects a Hindu's life.

Ashramas

According to Hindu teaching there are four **ashramas**—stages of life. The first stage is the student. From the age of about eight to about twenty, young people should study and learn about the religion. They are then ready to take their place as adults, and go on to the next stage, which is called **grihastha**. This is the householder stage, when a person is expected to earn a living, marry, and have a family. As they get older (some people think at about the age of 50), they are expected to leave friends and family behind and go and live on their own in a place where they can have peace and quiet. This is the stage called **vanaprastha**. They should give up all kinds of pleasure because the idea is to begin to prepare to leave the body at death. Anything that gives the body pleasure should therefore be left behind, and the person should begin to concentrate only on their religion. The last stage is that of the holy man, or **sannyasin**. A sannyasin has no fixed home and as few possessions as possible—usually just the clothes he wears and a bowl for his food. He has no responsibilities or family ties, so he is able to concentrate entirely on his religion.

Although this is the ideal life, many Hindus cannot afford to live their lives like this, or do not wish to do so. For all but a few Hindus, the student years end long before the age of twenty. Many Hindus do not wish to give up everything they enjoy in their lives, and so continue in the grihastha stage until they die. Only a few Hindus go on to the third stage, and even fewer become sannyasins.

The idea of the four stages of life is based on the most important Hindu teaching that the aim of everyone's life is moksha—joining with Brahman. This can only be achieved when the person is no longer affected by things in the world—in other words, is ready to give up the world. By the time he reaches the stage of the sannyasin, a Hindu has had sufficient experience of the world to be able to judge the best and worst of life. They can therefore decide on the basis of experience whether or not they want to give up the world.

A sannyasin.

Cows are allowed to wander where they like.

Respect for all life

Hindus respect all life because of their belief in reincarnation. This means that many Hindus— though not all – are vegetarians. They do not eat meat because they believe that it is important to respect the life of animals. Even if they eat other kinds of meat, traditionally, no Hindu will eat beef. This is because to a Hindu, the cow is sacred. No one really knows the reason for this, but it is probably partly because the white cow is a symbol of atman—the soul that is present in everything. In India, cows are protected because they are sacred. They are milked, and cow dung is used as a fertilizer and is often dried to use as fuel, but cows themselves are never killed for food. They are allowed to wander wherever they like, even in towns and cities. There are severe punishments for killing a cow, even in an accident.

THE COW

This passage shows why the cow is so important for Hindus.

> Cow protection is the dearest possession of the Hindu heart. No one who does not believe in cow protection can possibly be a Hindu. It is noble belief. Cow worship means to me worship of innocence, protection of the weak and helpless, brotherhood between man and beast. The cow was in India the best companion. She was the giver of plenty. Protection of the cow means protection of the whole dumb creation of God.

My religion, M. K. Gandhi

NEW WORDS

Ashrama Stage of life. Hindus believe there are four.
Grihastha Second stage of life— householder.
Sannyasin Holy man.
Vanaprastha The third stage of life.

27

FESTIVALS 1

This section tells you about the festival of Divali.

Hindu calendars are based on the changes in the moon. Most Hindu festivals take place in the middle of the month when the moon is full, or at the very end when it is just about to return as the new moon. India is an enormous country, and it is important to remember that festivals are not celebrated in the same way in different parts of the country. They may also be celebrated differently by Hindus living in other parts of the world. In particular, the same festival may be used by different groups of Hindus to remember different stories. For almost all Hindus, Divali is the most important festival in the year.

Divali

Divali takes place at the end of the month of Ashwin, and carries on into the month of Kartik (October–November in the Western calendar). In some places it is a three-day festival, but it usually lasts for five days. It includes the beginning of the financial year.

"Divali" is from the Sanskrit *dipavali*, meaning collection of lights. Throughout the festival Hindus decorate their homes, mandirs, and other buildings with rows of lights. Today, small electric lights are often used.

Like many other Hindu festivals, Divali remembers several different stories. One of the most popular stories is from the *Ramayana*. It tells how Prince Rama won the battle against his enemies and found his wife Sita. They returned home and Rama was crowned king. Lamps were lit for Rama's victory procession. There are also stories about how the god Vishnu won a battle with the wicked giant Narakasura, and how he tricked a king named Bali who was trying to take over the world. In different parts of India, people think that some of these stories are more important than others, so the festival is celebrated in different ways in different places.

Lighting candles for Divali.

Divali is also a time for remembering Lakshmi, the goddess who brings good fortune. She is supposed to visit houses that are clean and neat, and some people think that the divas are to light her way. She brings good luck throughout the coming year. For people who own stores and businesses, this is especially important, because they believe that Lakshmi helps their businesses do well. Divali comes at the end of the financial year, so they make sure that their account books are up to date and that all their debts are paid. They can then start the new year well and hope that, with Lakshmi's help, it will be a good one.

Divali is a family festival. People give each other presents and share meals with friends and relations. Sending cards for Divali is becoming more popular, especially with Hindus who live in the West. There are fire-work displays and bonfires, with singing and dancing. The idea is to show that darkness can be driven away by light. This is a symbol that shows that evil can be driven away by good.

BALI AND VAMANA (THE DWARF)

This is one of the stories which Hidus remember at Divali.

Bali was a very powerful king, and began to oppress people. Vishnu came to earth as Vamana (a dwarf), and asked the king to give him as much land as he could cover in three strides. Bali laughed and granted the wish. Vishnu changed into an enormous figure, and took one stride that covered the sky, and one that covered the earth. With the third stride he pushed Bali into the underworld. However, Vishnu declared that people should remember how generous Bali had been by celebrating a festival in his honor —Divali.

Divali celebrations at a temple.

FESTIVALS II

This section tells you about a festival for Krishna's birthday and festivals that honor the goddess Durga.

Janmashtami

Janmashtami takes place in Shravan, which usually falls in August in the Western calendar. It celebrates the birthday of the god Krishna. The stories about Krishna say that he was born at midnight, so many Hindus spend all night in the temple. At midnight, there is singing and dancing before everyone shares specially cooked desserts. In many temples, a nonstop reading of the Bhagavad Gita is organized for the eight days and nights before the festival. It takes about three hours to read the Bhagavad Gita all the way through, so a list of people is needed, with reserves in case anyone is ill. The reading is timed to finish at midnight on Krishna's birthday.

Navaratri

Navaratri takes place in the month of Ashwin, which is September–October in the Western calendar. Its name means "nine-nights," which is the length of the festival. Like other Hindu festivals, it is used by different groups of Hindus to remember different stories, but most of the celebrations are to honor the Mother Goddess. She is called by several different names. (See page 10.) For Navaratri, she is remembered as Durga, a fierce soldier who rides into battle on a lion. Anyone who worships Durga as a special goddess keeps the festival with great care. This person often eats only one meal a day for the nine days of the festival. Although she is fierce, Durga is also thought to care for people, and so she is the symbol of mothers. In the story of the Ramayana, Prince Rama prays to Durga for help when his wife Sita has been captured. This means that Navaratri is an important time for families. In particular, girls

A baby Krishna murti in a cradle—part of a temple celebration for Janmashtami.

who have been married during the past year try to return home at this time. They are given presents. In northern India, there are open-air plays during the festival acting out parts of the Ramayana story to remind people of it. In other places, people dance around a shrine of Durga, which may be specially built for the festival.

Dassehra

Dassehra and Navaratri are sometimes put together as the same festival. *Dassehra* means tenth day, and it falls on the day after the end of Navaratri. During Navaratri, God is worshiped through a murti of Durga. At Dassehra, this murti is taken to the nearest river and washed. Hindus believe that as it disappears under the water, it takes all their unhappiness and bad luck with it. This makes Dassehra a very happy festival.

Dassehra also makes us remember the story in the Ramayana of the battle between Prince Rama and the evil demon, Ravana. Rama won the battle with the help of his brother and Hanuman,

Ravana, Dassehra celebrations in Delhi.

the monkey king, because Durga was on his side. In many places, bonfires and statues of Ravana are burned. In Delhi, the capital of India, there is an enormous fireworks display at Dassehra. The main part of the celebrations is the burning of a wooden statue of Ravana measuring 98 feet (30 m) in height.

Like all Hindu festivals, there is a serious lesson behind all the enjoyment. The story of the Ramayana is the story of how good wins over the powers of evil, and reminds people of God's love. During Dassehra, Hindus try to make up any quarrels they may have had during the past year.

WORSHIP OF DURGA

This is part of a passage in the Scriptures that describes the goddess Durga. It helps to explain why Durga is such an important goddess.

Durga pervades the world. She creates, maintains, and destroys it as the need arises. Although Durga is eternal, she appears again and again to protect the world. She supports and shelters all beings. As "shakambhari" she provides the world with food.

From the *Devi Mahatmya* in the *Markandeya Purana*

FESTIVALS III

This section tells you about other Hindu celebrations.

Holi

Holi is a spring festival. It is celebrated by Hindus all over the world, although they remember different stories in their celebrations. Many Hindus remember stories about when Krishna was young. He often used to play tricks on people, so Holi is a time for practical jokes. A favorite trick with children is to throw colored powders and water over people in the streets. There are often water fights as people join in the fun.

A more serious story gives the festival its name. Holika was a princess who tried to kill Prahlada, a great follower of Vishnu. Prahlada was saved because he chanted the names of God. This story reminds Hindus how important it is to trust God.

Raksha Bandhan

At Raksha Bandhan, a sister ties a colored silk or cotton bracelet around her brother's wrist.

She hopes that it will protect him, and it is a sign that he will protect her. The custom recalls the story of the god Indra, who was attacked by an evil demon. He was saved because his wife had tied a magic string around his wrist.

Ramnavami

Ramnavami is the birthday festival of the god Rama. Rama is a very popular god for Hindus, and he is often worshiped at the shrines in people's homes. If they can, Hindus go to the temple for Ramnavami to worship there, too. There are readings from the Ramayana. A special part of the worship is the singing of the Ramanama, which is a list of all the names of Rama.

Like many other Hindu festivals, Ramnavami is a day of **fasting**. For Hindus fasting means going without certain foods. These are foods like meat, fish, onions, garlic, rice, and wheat. Foods that are allowed on fast days are things like fresh fruit, milk, and ghee. Most eat these simple foods in order to make a sacrifice. They give up both meat and fish, and the common staples in their diet, such as rice and wheat.

Raksha Bandhan.

Special patterns are made at New Year.

New Year

Hindus may celebrate New Year at different times, depending on where in India they live or came from. The beginning of the calendar year is different from the beginning of the financial year. Whenever New Year occurs, it is always seen as the chance to turn over a new leaf and make changes in your life. Families get up very early, and often make special puja. Houses are cleaned and often painted, and everyone wears new or clean clothes. Colored chalks or flours are used to make patterns on the floor, which Hindus hope will bring happiness throughout the year to come.

Hindus celebrate many other festivals. Some are important in a particular area or to worshipers of a particular god. Most festivals involve making special puja, and many involve fasting.

A PRAYER TO RAMA

This is part of a prayer to Rama.

> May Rama, the descendant of King Raghu, protect my head.
>
> May Rama, the son of King Dasharatha, protect my temples.
>
> May Rama, the son of Queen Kausalya, protect my eyes.
>
> May Rama, the pupil of Vishwamitra, protect my ears.
>
> May Rama, the affectionate brother of Lakshmana, protect my mouth.

NEW WORD

Fast Go without food for religious reasons.

HINDU HISTORY

This section tells you something about the history of Hinduism.

Hinduism is now the religion of most people who live in India, and the history of the country and the religion are very closely connected.

How Hinduism began

Hinduism did not "begin." It developed gradually over many hundreds and even thousands of years. About 4,000 years ago, the people who lived in what today is called India worshiped many gods from the world around them. They were gods like fire, water, and wind. Then the northern part of the country was taken over by invaders, who brought their religion with them. This involved worship of the sun, moon, and sky. Over many years, these two religions gradually joined together. People did not stop worshiping their own gods, but they began worshiping other gods, too. Over hundreds of years, the idea developed that these gods were not really different beings, but different ways of looking at the same thing. They were all ways of showing Brahman, the Great Power.

Hinduism stayed like this for hundreds of years. Then people became dissatisfied, and began to think that other religions had more to offer, especially the new system of thought begun by Gautama, the Buddha. Under the **Buddhist** emperor Asoka, in the third century BCE, almost the whole of India was Buddhist. Hinduism had to change. The Vedas and stories like the Ramayana and the Mahabharata were written down, so they became easier to remember and retell. Important teachers spent their lives teaching about these and other stories. People began to learn the lessons behind the stories. Hindu beliefs gradually became clearer, and Hinduism became popular again.

How Hinduism developed

Between the eighth and sixteenth centuries CE, India was invaded three times. This time the invaders were **Muslims**, followers of the religion of Islam. They ruled India for 300 years after the third invasion. They did not like some of the ways that Hindus worshiped, and destroyed many Hindu temples. During the time they ruled India, Hinduism became less popular because many people became Muslims.

The next rulers of India were the British. They began as traders but gradually took over more and more power, and became full rulers of the country in 1857. For the next one hundred years, they controlled India. In that time there

Havan, offering to the god of fire, is still an important part of Hindu worship.

Muslim refugees crowding a train from Delhi to Pakistan in 1947.

were many changes. Hinduism had to change, too, as some of the old ideas were challenged. During the nineteenth century, important teachers like Vivekananda began presenting Hinduism as a world religion. In the twentieth century, the Hindu leader Mahatma Gandhi was one of the most important people to shape the history of the country.

When India became independent in 1947, the country was divided. A new country called Pakistan was created, to be a Muslim country. Many Hindus who were living in that area moved back to India. Many Muslims living in India moved to Pakistan. It was a time of great suffering and bitterness, and thousands of people were killed in riots. Since that time, India has been mainly Hindu.

Hinduism is a mixture of many different beliefs and customs. They have come together over thousands of years to make one religion. This is one reason why Hinduism is a very tolerant religion and accepts many different views.

Hindus say that all religions are a search for truth, and everyone has to find out the truth for himself or herself.

NEW WORDS

Buddhist Follower of Buddhism.
Muslim Follower of the religion of Islam.

HINDU TEACHING

This passage from the Hindu Scriptures shows what Hindus aim to achieve.

> *Even as a mirror of gold, covered by dust, when cleaned well shines again in full splendor, when a man has seen the Truth of the Spirit he is one with him, the aim of his life is fulfilled, and he is ever beyond sorrow. Then the soul of a man becomes a lamp by which he finds the truth of Brahman. Then he sees God, pure, never-born, everlasting; and when he sees God he is free from all bondage.*

Svetasvatara Upanishad 2

THE CASTE SYSTEM

This section tells you about the different groups of people in India.

Hinduism teaches that different people have different abilities. What these are depends mainly on their previous lives. Hinduism also teaches that it is important for each person to make the most of their abilities. This led to an idea that particular groups of people had particular talents, and for hundreds of years,

people in India have been divided into groups. These groups are called **varnas**, and they have been an important part of the way the country of India has been organized. There are four main groups, and at first they were probably quite separate.

The first and most important group were **Brahmins**. They were best at being priests, and jobs that involve giving advice. The second group were **Kshatriyas**, who were soldiers and people who rule the country. The **Vaishyas** were storekeepers, traders, and farmers. The lowest of the four were the **Shudras**, who were servants for the other three groups. Gradually, these groups divided into many smaller groups called **jatis,** or **castes.** Your jati depends on your job. Jobs are passed on in families, so a son usually does the same job as his father. Different jatis are higher or lower than others. People in higher jatis are thought to be more pure than those in lower jatis. Today, some people are still very strict about groups that are thought to be less pure than their own. This is especially true when marriage is being considered. For example, they will not marry someone from a lower jati.

Brahmins

The highest group are Brahmins, and Hindu priests usually come from this group. Today, many Brahmins do other jobs. The fact that they are the highest group means that Brahmins tend to keep the rules about caste more strictly than other Hindus. For example, a Brahmin cannot eat certain foods unless the foods have been cooked by another Brahmin, and they are not supposed to drink alcohol.

Priests are usually Brahmins.

Harijans

The lowest group of all in Hinduism are the **Harijans**. They are below the other four groups, and do the dirtiest jobs. For example, many Harijans work with leather, which no "higher" Hindu would do. For many years, other Hindus would not have anything to do with Harijans. They were called **"untouchables."** In the early years of the twentieth century, the Hindu leader Gandhi worked hard to improve the lives of untouchables. He gave them the name Harijans, which means children of God.

This way of dividing people into groups is called the **caste system.** It is the way that people in India have lived for hundreds of years. In the past 50 years, things have changed. More people travel away from their home area, and live and work in cities. In factories and shops, they have to meet and talk with people who are not from their own group. The rules cannot be kept so strictly. Now many Brahmins are not priests, not all members of the army are Kshatriyas, and many people who are not Vaishyas own shops. Apart from Brahmins and Harijans, many people are not very interested in what varna they

are, but they know what jati they belong to, and what this means in their dealings with other people. Since 1947, it has been against the law in India to treat former untouchables differently, but it takes a long time to change the way people think, and changes in the law are not always enough. In many villages in India the caste system is still very strict, especially when it comes to marriage.

NEW WORDS

Brahmins Priests (first varna).
Caste Another name for a jati.
Caste system Name given to the organization of varnas and jatis.
Harijans Gandhi's name for untouchables.
Jati Part of a varna.
Kshatriyas Second varna.
Shudras Fourth varna.
Untouchables Lowest group of people.
Vaishyas Third varna.
Varna One of four main groups.

THE DUTIES OF THE VARNAS

This passage shows how the duties of different varnas go back to the law books of Hinduism.

A Kshatriya's first duty is to protect people and property. Agriculture, banking, commerce, and dairy farming are suitable occupations for a Vaishya. Serving the three twice-born varnas is the duty of a Shudra. If a Shudra cannot get a good living by service, he may become a tradesman or learn a craft, but he should always serve the upper varnas.

Yajnavalkya 1.119–21

Mahatma Gandhi

This section tells you about a famous Hindu.

One of the most important Hindus in the last hundred years was a man called Mohandas Karamchand Gandhi. He was an important leader in India when the country was becoming independent, and he did much to shape the way Hindus thought about themselves.

Gandhi's early life

Mohandas Gandhi was born on October 2, 1869, in a small town in western India. He was the youngest son in the family. Although they were not high in the caste system, his family was important in the local area, and they were quite well-off. Gandhi's parents were strict Hindus, and he was brought up to worship Vishnu.

As a boy, Gandhi was very shy and timid. He did not do particularly well at school because of this. In those days, marriages between children were common in India, and when he was thirteen, Gandhi's parents arranged his marriage to a girl called Kasturbai. At first, he and his wife did not get along well, and because he was at school they spent more time apart than they were together. As they grew up, however, they became very close.

When Gandhi was sixteen his father died, and the family became short of money. He had to find some way of earning his living, and a friend suggested he should go to England to study law. At first his family was against the idea, but he persuaded them, and Kasturbai sold her jewelry to buy his ticket. After three years in London, he passed his exams, and returned to India in 1891.

Gandhi's work

Back in India, life was difficult, and after two years he was offered a chance to go and work in South Africa. There he began to realize that "Coloreds" were being treated unfairly. This is called **discrimination**. (The term "Coloreds" is used for people of mixed race in South Africa.) When his law work was finished, he decided to stay in South Africa to try to improve the way Indians were being treated there. He worked there for the next twenty years. He became well-known as a writer, and fighter for freedom. His idea of fighting was not the same as other people's, however. He said that violence was wrong, and instead he talked about **ahimsa**—nonviolence and respect for life. He taught that it is important to stand up for what you believe, but this does not mean that you have to fight for it with violence.

Gandhi with his wife in 1913.

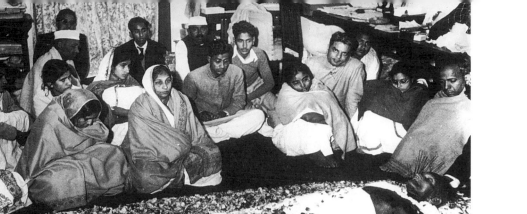

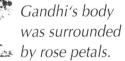

Gandhi's body was surrounded by rose petals.

By the time Gandhi went back to India in 1915, he was very well known. A famous Indian poet called him "Great Soul," and for the rest of his life he was known by the Indian word for this—**Mahatma**. He began working to improve life for the millions of people in India who were very poor. He said it was wrong to call people "untouchable," and he gave them the new name "Harijan," which means "children of God."

Gandhi played an important part in the talks about India becoming independent, and did his best to calm the fighting and riots between Hindus and Muslims when the new country of Pakistan was created. Some Hindus felt so strongly that Pakistan should not have been created that they wanted to fight to try to win it back. They knew that Gandhi would never agree to this. A man called Nathuram Godse decided that the only answer was to get rid of Gandhi. On January 30, 1948, when Gandhi was on his way to a prayer meeting in Delhi, Godse shot him three times. Gandhi died at once. His

funeral took place the next day, and over three million people took part in the funeral procession. Today, Gandhi is remembered and respected as a man of peace not only by Hindus, but by people all over the world.

GRIEF FOR GANDHI

This is part of the radio broadcast made by the Indian Prime Minister when Gandhi was killed.

The light has gone out of our lives and there is darkness everywhere. Our beloved leader, Bapu, as we called him, the father of the nation, is no more. The light has gone out, I said, and yet I was wrong. For the light that shone in this country was no ordinary light. In a thousand years that light will still be seen ... for it represented the living, the eternal truths, reminding us of the right path, drawing us from error, taking this ancient country to freedom.

Jawaharlal Nehru, January 30,1948

NEW WORDS

Ahimsa Nonviolence.
Discrimination Treating someone unfairly.
Mahatma "Great soul" (title given to Gandhi).

HINDUS IN THE UNITED STATES

This section tells you something about Hindus in the United States.

Until the late twentieth century, Hinduism was almost completely unknown to most Americans. The first Hindu to be known in the U.S. was Swami Vivekanada, the Hindu representative at the World Parliament of Religions in Chicago in 1893.

Today there are about 910,000 Hindus in the United States. Most of these live in or near cities like New York, Washington, Chicago, and Los Angeles.

In India, praying and worshiping as part of a group is not something that happens very often except at some of the major temples. For Hindus living in the U.S., meeting other people who share the same religion and background is important, so they have started to meet together for worship. They often gather for worship on Sundays because this fits the American lifestyle. Most temples in the U.S. are dedicated to Krishna or Rama.

Inside a Hindu temple in a Western country.

Some Hindu temples in the West are in buildings that have been altered.

Hinduism is based in the home. When most of the people around are not followers of Hinduism, this becomes even more important. Children learn their religion from the way their parents follow it. As in India, every Hindu home in the United States has a shrine. If the family can afford it, this is a separate room. If not, it can be just a shelf on the wall, usually in the kitchen or a bedroom. Family puja takes place there, just as it does in India.

Hindu women

Hindu women are highly respected. Hindus believe that the most important job a woman can do is to run the house and look after the family. Some Hindu women are encouraged to have a good education, and in the United States many are doctors and teachers.

Hare Krishna

Hindus do not usually persuade other people to join their religion, but Hinduism has gained a lot of interest from people in the West. Many people have joined groups led by **gurus**. A guru is a religious leader, often a man who teaches about a particular part of Hinduism. One of the groups most often seen in the U.S. is usually called Hare Krishna. This is the name given to followers of the guru called **Swami** Prabhupada. (Swami is a title used for Hindu holy men.) He began the International Society for Krishna Consciousness (ISKCON) in 1967, and all its temples are run by Westerners who have **converted** to Hinduism. Swami Prabhupada explained Hindu teachings about finding your real self by saying that most people live their lives as if they were asleep. When people are asleep, they forget what they are like when they are awake. In the same way, most people do not know what they really are, and need to wake up to find their real selves. Swami Prabhupada said that the way to do this was to repeat a mantra of the names of Krishna. This becomes a form of meditation. Followers of Hare Krishna believe that everything they do in their lives is an offering to Krishna. They live strictly and simply. There are members of the group in some cities, easily recognized by their yellow robes.

A Hare Krishna procession in the West.

NEW WORDS

Convert To become a member of a religion.
Guru Religious teacher.
Swami Title given to Hindu holy men.

A PRAYER AT THE END OF PUJA

Grant me, O Lord, a healthy appearance, success in my work, and destroy my enemies. May I be blessed with sons, riches, and all creature comforts.

You are my mother and father, my brother and friend. You are my knowledge and my strength. You are indeed my entire existence, O Lord.

Whatever actions I perform with my body, speech, mind, and other sense organs, whatever I do knowingly or as a habit, I offer it all, without any reservations to Narayana.

From the *Puranas*

SPECIAL OCCASIONS I

This section tells you about important things that happen to young Hindus.

The special ceremonies that are performed throughout a Hindu's life are called **samskars**. Altogether, there are sixteen samskars that are performed at various times during a person's life. Hindus hope that these ceremonies will improve the person's karma, his or her place in the cycle of rebirth. Like most important Hindu ceremonies, the correct way of performing them is laid down in the Scriptures.

Before birth

Even before a baby is expected, the couple pray about the kind of child they would like. The first three samskars are performed during pregnancy. They are prayers that God will protect the mother and the baby, so that the child will be born healthy.

Birth

When the baby is born, he or she is washed, and then their father places a tiny droplet of honey and ghee in the baby's mouth, using a

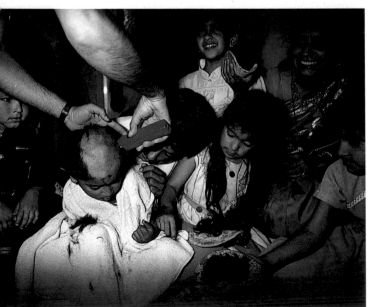

gold ring. Then he recites a prayer from the Scriptures. In some places, the sacred syllable "Oum" is written on the baby's tongue with honey, using a special pen. This is the syllable that begins all prayers, so it is like saying that the baby's life will be a prayer. For most Hindus it is important to note the exact time and place of birth, since this will be used by the priest who prepares the baby's **horoscope**. A horoscope is a way of telling the future based on the positions of the stars. Many Hindus use horoscopes in their lives to find out the best time for events to take place.

The naming ceremony

The baby is given its name at a special ceremony, usually when it is twelve days old. Choosing the name is very important, because the right name will bring the child good luck. A priest is often asked to suggest an initial or syllable that would be suitable. The baby is dressed in new clothes and placed in a cradle. The ceremony itself is very simple. The name is announced by the eldest woman in the family, and the baby's father says into the baby's ear, "Now your name is ... ." Songs are sung, and a special dessert made of fruit, nuts, and sugar is given to friends and relatives who have come to the ceremony.

The next three samskars take place as the child grows. The ninth samskar takes place with the baby's first haircut, which is usually when it is about a year old. For a boy, this means having his whole head shaved. It is a symbol of removing any bad karma from his previous life.

Shaving a boy's head is the ninth samskar.

A father giving the sacred thread to his son.

The thread ceremony

This is the tenth samskar and is a very important ceremony for boys in the three higher varnas. Members of the lower castes and female children do not have the right to take part in this ceremony. In India it usually takes place sometime between a boy's seventh and twelfth birthdays. The sacred thread—a loop of cotton—is hung over the left shoulder, so that it hangs down to the right hip. Once he has been given this thread, a boy is counted as a man. He can read the Vedas and carry out religious ceremonies. He wears the thread for the rest of his life, changing it at festivals.

A guru prepares the boy for this ceremony, and prays for the boy before he is given the thread. Then he becomes the boy's teacher while the boy studies the Scriptures. Some boys spend several years studying. The thread ceremony is the time when a boy joins the religion, so it is the reason why members of the three highest

varnas are sometimes called "twice-born." They have had a spiritual or religious birth, in addition to a physical one.

CELEBRATING THE BIRTH OF A BABY

This is part of the prayer that the father recites to a newborn baby.

> *Dear child, I give you this honey and ghee, which is provided by God, who is the creator of the world. May you be protected by God and live in this world for a hundred autumns. By God's grace may you become strong and firm like a rock, an axe for the wicked, and bright in character. May God give you long life and understanding of the Vedas.*

Grihya Sutra

NEW WORDS

Horoscope Way of telling the future based on the stars.
Samskars Ceremonies of life.

SPECIAL OCCASIONS II

This section tells you about Hindu teachings on marriage. Customs vary from one part of India to another, and from caste to caste.

Hindus think it is important to marry, so that there can be children who can carry on the family. Parents usually choose who their children will marry. They are thought to know best, because they have had more life experience. This is called an **arranged marriage**. The parents often take the advice of a priest and may use the couple's horoscopes to make sure that they are well matched. In the past, couples did not meet until their wedding day. Today, things are not as strict as they once were, and the couple may suggest a possible partner, or have met a few times.

The first step of a Hindu marriage is the ceremony to announce the engagement. The men from both families meet. There are readings from the Vedas, and prayers are said. The ceremony ends with a meal.

The wedding

The wedding ceremony usually lasts about an hour, but the celebrations often go on for days. The wedding takes place either in a temple or the bride's home. The bride wears special eye makeup, and a dye is used to make patterns on her hands and feet. She wears a new red and gold **sari**, and gold jewelry. Preparing the bride for the ceremony takes several hours. Both the bride and groom wear garlands of flowers.

The first part of the wedding is when the bride's father welcomes the bridegroom. The bridegroom sits under a special canopy, which is a decorated covering. He is given small presents that are symbols of happiness and a good life. Then the bride arrives, usually wearing a veil so her face cannot be seen. She removes this during the ceremony. The couple sit in front of a special

A Hindu bride wears beautiful jewelry.

fire. Their right hands are tied together and holy water is sprinkled on them when the bride's father "gives" her to the bridegroom. There are prayers and offerings of rice.

The most important part of the ceremony is when the bride and groom take seven steps

The couple's right hands are tied together.

The bride and groom sit under a special canopy.

towards the fire. At each step they stop and make promises to each other. While they do this, they are joined by a piece of cloth. It is hung loosely round the bridegroom's neck and tied to the bride's sari. This is a symbol that they are being joined as husband and wife. Once they have taken the steps together, they are married. There are more prayers and readings, and flower petals are thrown before the guests give the wedding presents. Then there will be a feast. After she is married, the bride is thought of as belonging to her husband's family.

Divorce

Indian law allows divorce, but strict Hindus do not accept any ending of a marriage except death. It is seen as a disgrace to both families if the couple divorces.

THE MARRIAGE MANTRA

These words are said as the bride and groom take the seven steps during the wedding ceremony.

> *My bride, follow me in my vows. Take the first step for food, take the second step for strength, the third for increasing prosperity, the fourth for happiness, the fifth for children. May we have healthy and long-lived sons. Take the sixth step for seasonal pleasures, take the seventh step for friendship.*

Ashwalayana Grihya Sutra

NEW WORDS

Arranged marriage Marriage where the partners are chosen or suggested by relatives.
Sari Long piece of cloth worn as a dress.

SPECIAL OCCASIONS III

This section tells you about what happens when a Hindu dies.

Hindus believe in rebirth, so they think that the body is not needed after death. Death is seen as being a welcome release from life, so a funeral is a time for looking forward, as well as a time of sadness because the person is no longer with people who love them. India is a hot country, so it is the custom for Hindu funerals to be on the day after death, before the body decays.

Hindu funerals

When someone dies, their body is washed and wrapped in a cloth called a **shroud**. A garland of flowers is often placed on the body, and it is put on a special stretcher. Then it is taken to be cremated. It is placed on a special fire called a **funeral pyre**. If possible, the funeral pyre is built on a ghat by one of the sacred rivers. A ghat is a special platform at the bottom of steps leading to the river. If there is no running water, there is a cremation ground outside every town or village.

The eldest son walks around the funeral pyre three times carrying a lighted torch, then he sets the pyre on fire. Ghee is used to help the flames burn. Families who can afford it include blocks of sandalwood in the pyre, which burn with a sweet smell. The people say prayers, and there are readings from the Scriptures reminding the mourners that everyone who dies will be reborn. The closest male relative stays at the pyre until the fire has gone out, then he collects the ashes. All Hindus hope that they will be in Varanasi when they die, and that their ashes will be scattered on the Ganges River. They believe that this will save them many future rebirths.

In many Indian cities, and for Hindus living in the West, bodies are not burned in the open air but are taken to a **crematorium**. Important customs like walking around the body with a lighted torch are carried out at the undertakers. The ashes are collected after the body has been cremated. Many Hindus living in other countries have the ashes of their relatives flown back to India so that they can be scattered on the Ganges River.

A Hindu funeral arriving at a cremation ground.

Funeral ghats on the banks of the Ganges River at Varanasi.

The kriya ceremony

After the funeral, the relatives of the person who has died return home and bathe. Death is thought to make anyone who has been near the body unclean, so the relatives do not go out and meet people until all the ceremonies are over. The last ceremony takes place ten or twelve days after the funeral. It is called the **kriya ceremony**. Rice and milk are made into offerings. This is not just for the person who has died, but for everyone in the family who has died in the past. Rice is an important food, and milk comes from the sacred cow. Once this ceremony has been held, the person's soul is believed to have been rehoused in another body, so the family can return to normal.

NEW WORDS

Crematorium Place where dead bodies are burned.
Funeral pyre Pile of wood for burning a dead body.
Kriya ceremony Final ceremony after a death.
Shroud Piece of cloth wrapped around a dead body.

WORDS FOR A FUNERAL

These verses from the Scriptures are said to the body at a funeral.

The sages through penance won and increased their religious merit. May you go to them according to your penance.

Go to those who excelled in their penance and have achieved firm places in heaven, if your penance merits it.

Perhaps you will go to be among those who fought in battles and sacrificed their lives, or those who gave thousands of sacrificial gifts.

May this earth be a pleasant, thornless resting place for this departing soul and give him a happy refuge.

Arthava Veda 18.2.15–17,19

INDEX

The numbers in **bold** tell where the main definitions of the words are.